Contents

3

Introduction

In November 2000, Val Bowden sent me a pamphlet of her writing. Val had been a colleague of my wife at Cowbridge School in the Vale of Glamorgan, but took early retirement eight years after she was diagnosed with Parkinson's Disease. Cowbridge is regularly listed as the highest achieving secondary school in Wales, and one of the best in the UK.

Val was a highly respected music and special needs teacher. No longer able to play the piano, she has turned to writing and has tried to explore and share her experiences of the disease with her readers. The dialogues she wrote form the backbone of this book. Some examples of her poetry are also included, along with some of the best poets now working in the English language. Those poets have very generously agreed to support this publication and it is with particular pleasure that I was able to involve the Nobel Prize-winning poet, Seamus Heaney and the Poet Laureate, Andrew Motion. All of the poets in this book are writers I greatly admire; our thanks go to them and their publishers.

__Wading Through Deep Water__ brings together a remarkable combination of talents: I invited these friends and fellow poets to publish work on whatever subject; we were simply to bear in mind that the struggles of Val and others in illness, and the impulse of every real poem, share that human strength which works towards life-enhancement. The purpose of this book is to celebrate life in its light and dark moments. When reading and re-reading poetry, puzzlement and intrigue is the point. Poetry is not working necessarily to deliver an instant meaning. It's a cross between a prayer and a crossword puzzle, a sort of code for the soul.

Tony Curtis
Editor

Lynette Craig

Not a Poem

This is
not a poem -
but if you are prepared to wait
a poem could happen
unexpectedly -
a line at a time
maybe some rhyme -
it would settle
like a snowflake
on my tongue
and I would
speak it
for you.

Seamus Heaney

The Clothes Shrine

It was a whole new sweetness
In the early days to find
Light white muslin blouses
On a see-through nylon line
Drip-drying in the bathroom
Or a nylon slip in the shine
Of its own electricity –
As if St. Brigid once more
Had rigged up a ray of sun
Like the one she'd strung on air
To dry her own cloak on
(Hard-pressed Brigid, so
Unstoppably on the go) -
The damp and slump and unfair
Drag of the workaday
Made light of and got through
As usual, brilliantly.

AWARENESS

"Meg? Good gracious! What a lovely surprise! I haven't seen you for years. How are you? Come in."

"I'm fine, thank you. It's good to see you. I'm staying with my mother for a few days; she hasn't been too well. I thought it would be nice to see you after such a long time. I should have rung really. I hope it's convenient."

"Of course it is. I'm so pleased to see you."

"Gosh! You haven't changed much. I'd have recognised you anywhere - except for the hair - that gives our age away, doesn't it? How many years is it? It's a long time since I moved away."

"It is a long time; fourteen years at least. I haven't seen you since then, I'm sure. A lot of water has gone under the bridge in that time; nothing is for ever, is it?"

"Very true. I seem to remember that the last time we met, your arm was troubling you. Is it better now?"

"It's a long story. Have you got time for a coffee? It would be nice to have a chat and catch up on old times. Let me take your coat. Thank goodness you've caught me at a good time. I'm sorry to say that I'm not always like this."

"What do you mean? What's the matter?"

"I've got Parkinson's Disease. I've had it since 1988, probably before, only I didn't know it."

"Parkinson's Disease? Surely not, you're too young. I thought only old people had Parkinson's. An elderly aunt of mine had it. How do you feel? My Aunty Betty had a terrible time with it."

"I'm coping, though at times it's difficult to manage."

"I knew you hadn't been feeling too good before I left, but I didn't think it was anything serious."

"Nor did I. I'd been having problems with my right arm for about four years and I attended the orthopaedic clinic in the hospital for ages, having treatment for a frozen shoulder. I couldn't understand, though, why the pain was

7

in my arm and not the shoulder. I had cortisone injections, creams, manipulation under general anaesthetic, physiotherapy, and nothing worked."

"You have had a rough time, haven't you?"

"That's not all. I found I was slowing down a lot. Everything I did was as if in slow motion. I couldn't walk far, my legs felt heavy, I had terrible trouble turning over in bed, I had no strength to do chores round the house. And my handwriting! Writing and marking in school was getting beyond me. Oh, and another thing, my husband had noticed that I didn't swing my right arm any more, and I often held it up under my chin in strange positions."

"So the orthopaedic doctor diagnosed Parkinson's, did he?"

"No, indeed. After such a long time, I got desperate. I knew something was wrong; things weren't improving so I decided to ask for a second opinion."

"You must have been extremely worried."

"I certainly was. I was given a letter to take to a specialist. I rang and made the appointment. It was a private consultation so I didn't have to wait long; I saw him within a week. Straight away, the neurologist, - for that's what he was - told me it was Parkinson's. God, I felt sick. I couldn't think straight.
    He tried to explain it to me, but I couldn't take it in. He told me that he could tell as soon as set eyes on me. The way we look, walk and move our body is different. Of course, I can see that myself, now."

"Gosh, that must have been a shock. Did you know anything about it at that time?"

"No, I didn't. I had heard about it, of course, but like most serious complaints or illnesses, until they actually affect you or your family, you don't really know much about them. But, now I know more about it, I think my grandfather may have had it. There was no medication to help him in those days; his life was dreadful."

"Yes, I clearly remember going to your grandparents' house with you, years ago. I remember being more than a little frightened of the man in the corner who made strange noises."

"I'll never forget my grandfather. He was virtually unable to move; he sat in his chair in the corner for decades. Every movement was slow motion; he couldn't speak, except in grunts, but it was surprising how the family could understand the grunts.

8

He was an amazing man, such strength of character, such intelligence laid waste. People in my father's income bracket didn't have cars in those days so my grandfather was never taken out. In the summer, if it was a hot day, he would be helped outside and he would sit on the wall. This was his only contact with the outside world for forty years.

My grandmother couldn't cope with caring for him and she left him alone in the house for hours on end every day. He'd have to struggle to the bathroom - which, fortunately, was downstairs - gripping on to rails that had been placed along the walls. It would take him half an hour or more to travel the twelve yards there and back. He fell on many occasions, often into the empty bath, and there he would have to remain until somebody discovered him lying in awkward positions; he was dead weight and couldn't even get into a comfortable position. I discovered him on the floor or in the bath on several occasions.

His life must have been hell; all he had was a daily newspaper, a radio, a pot of tea left standing on the hob, and a plate of cheese to keep him going while my gran was out. He didn't have many visitors because he couldn't speak and his grunting frightened and embarrassed most people.

Nothing was done to help him. He was simply described as a paraplegic and left to get on with life. He was eighty-five when he died having spent nearly forty years sitting in his chair in the corner. Some life!"

"You're right. No person should have to live like that."

"And I remember a lady who lived opposite us when I was a child. I think she may also have had Parkinson's. Memories I have of her frequently worry me, even now, fifty years later.

She was doubled up, could barely move and her hands used to shake. She used to stand, dribbling, at her front door hoping to waylay any passer-by to go to the shop for her. I'd look out through our front window to see if she was waiting at her door, and if she was, I'd go out through the back door, go up the road so that I could start to run, building up speed so that when passing her house it seemed I didn't know that she was there. I must have been horrid!"

"I shouldn't feel too badly about it. You were so young and had no conception of the problem."

"Maybe you're right. But I shan't forget her."

Barbara Bentley

Stranded

Early morning, and the sun's already melting tar.
Gulls squabble in a paradise sky,
too smooth, too blue. We pass the empty café
and its shanty-town hoardings – ice-cream,
minerals, hot pies, teas – then down the steps
from the fortified wall where the sea once escaped,
gutting houses, roaring down the road.

You know the currents here. You know how far
you can go without fear of being stranded.
Some fools walk out at the wrong time,
ignoring the tide that starts
as an arc of silver, a lucky horseshoe -
and yet, the channels fill so quickly.
Those who don't know, get caught.

But you're sure you can make it to that wreck
and back. You point to the husk of a boat
that was sucked under once, and is beached
at low tide. The heat plays tricks, so it's hard
to make out what we're heading for – gallows,
outpost, or heathen stone. The slab we reach
is dark and barnacled, hardly a hull.

We stretch in its shade, our rucksacks
like wreaths on the scorched remains
of buried hands on deck. I want warm pop
and sandwiches, fake fun to warn off ghosts
and the threat of your face eclipsed by the sun,
coming in close, your mouth full of salt
while water curves round us, a spittle glint.

Gillian Clarke

The Piano

The last bus sighs through the stops of the sleeping suburb
and he's home with a click of keys, a step on the stairs.
I see him again, shut in the upstairs sitting-room
in that huge Oxfam overcoat, one hand shuffling
through the music, the other lifting the black wing.

My light's out in the room he was born in. In the hall
the clock clears its throat and counts twelve hours
into space. His scales rise, falter and fall back -
not easy to fly on one wing, even for him
with those two extra digits he was born with.

I should have known there'd be music as he flew, singing,
and the midwife cried out, 'Magic fingers.' A small variation,
born with more, like obsession. They soon fell,
tied like the cord, leaving a small scar fading
on each hand like a memory of flight.

Midnight arpeggios, Bartok, Schubert. I remember,
kept in after school, the lonely sound of a piano lesson
through an open window between–times, sun on the lawn
and everyone gone, the piece played over and over
to the metronome of tennis. Sometimes in the small hours,

after 2, the hour of his birth, I lose myself listening
to that little piece by Schubert, perfected in the darkness
of space where the stars are so bright they cast shadows,
and I wait for that waterfall of notes, as if
two hands were not enough.

Michael Longley

The Lizard

At the restaurant on the road to Pisa airport
The only thing under the pergola to distract me
From gnocchi stuffed with walnuts in porcini sauce
Was a greeny lizard curving her belly like a bowl
So that when she tucked her hind legs behind her
In philosophical fashion and lifted up her hands
As though at prayer or in heated *conversazione,*
She wouldn't scorch her elegant fingers or toes
On the baking concrete and would feel the noon
As no more than a hot buckle securing her eggs.
We left the restaurant on the road to Pisa airport
And flew between Mont Blanc and the Matterhorn.
His lady co-pilot, the captain of our Boeing
Coyly let us know, specialised in smooth landings.

Les Murray

Reclaim the Sites

We are spared the Avenues of Liberation
and the water-cannoned Fifths of May
but I tire of cities clogged with salutes
to other cities: York, Liverpool, Oxford Streets
and memorial royalty: Elizabeth,
Albert, William, unnumbered George.
Give me Sally Huckstepp Road, ahead of
sepia Sussex, or Argyle, or Yankee numbering
- and why not a whole metropolis
street-signed for its own life and ours:
Childsplay Park and First Bra Avenue,
Unsecured Loan, the Boulevard Kiss,
Radar Strip, Bread Fragrance Corner,
Fumbletrouser, Delight Bridge, Timeless Square?

*"Sally Huckstepp was a Sydney woman who got drowned in a park for objecting when a corrupt police
inspector shot her criminal boyfriend execution style."*

CHANGES

"A lovely cup of coffee. I enjoyed that; I was parched. Tell me, are you still teaching? You must be coming up to retirement age now, surely? You are just a few months younger than I am, if I remember correctly."

"No, unfortunately, I'm not teaching now. I retired in 1996. I managed to keep going for 8 years after being told I had Parkinson's, but things were getting progressively worse. I found marking books difficult; comments about my pupils' work were impossible to write and completing end of term reports was a real bind. I don't know how the parents understood a word. Strangely, though, I could write on the board quite well, but, eventually, that went too. I could still play the piano, for a while, but I can't even do that now."

"I bet you missed working, didn't you? You were always so keen."

"I did miss it, definitely. But I felt it wasn't fair to my pupils. I taught children with special needs, a job demanding a special relationship between teacher and pupil. My speech was deteriorating; they were having problems understanding me and I was so lifeless and slow, lacking the enthusiasm and ability to stimulate them; things were difficult, to say the least.

As well as being a class teacher I was head of a year group, leading a team of seven form teachers, overseeing pastoral matters for nearly 200 pupils. I was unable to do my job as competently as I wished, having to depend on the goodwill of my teaching colleagues for their support and understanding. Teaching is hard enough without having to help out a colleague who's finding the going difficult.

I took early retirement on health grounds, but I must say that even now, after a few years of retirement, I still miss school very much."

"How did you come to terms with knowing that you had Parkinson's?"

"Very well, I suppose, on the whole. I felt very alone, though. It takes some time to accept that life is going to change and to find the means to adjust. Work was very important to me. If I had been home all day long as well, the time would have been interminable. I'd have had too much time to worry about my condition. My body seemed to be changing so much, I simply couldn't do things as quickly or as well as I used to. It made me think what life is all about, the uncertainty of the future and what's going to happen next."

"I know what you mean. Gosh, look at the time; I'd better go. It's been lovely to see you. I'm going home tomorrow, my mother is coming with me for a few weeks. We must keep in touch from now on. I'll give you a ring."

14

Pamela Johnson

Sea Dreams

Back to back, lazing in the dunes
three sisters after their swim, uniform
in navy bathing suits, their skin
itchy as salt water dries in the August sun.

The middle one reclines, eyes the horizon
where smoke like hair sways from a liner.
Herself on deck. Quoits. Dinner with the Captain.
Dancing her way to Rio.

Looking inland, the young one hugs her knees, tracks
the headland path, she'll stride it later.
She traces the arc of gulls, wheeling
to their nest in a crack of rock.

The eldest, cross-legged, eyes down, studies
the tight curve on the hook
of a black crab claw, notes the way a fly
feasts on a pie crust.

This is how the days pass
each sister longing
for the evening cool
of their separate rooms.

Catherine Fisher

At Pompeii

1.

It's no good trying to imagine who I was,
what my last thoughts were.
I have no spaces for dreams;
lie in a huddled heap, one arm sprawled out.
Nikons click at me all day;
in the night when only dogs prowl
and wind stirs the pines
I don't sit up and walk. On the last
day I won't be moving either. Save
your efforts for some real calamity;
this one's too old and too choked up with time;
years have fallen on it in a silent silt.
Real bodies lie now under new
volcanoes and in streets
not unlike these; say about them
what should be said. If you're up to it.
I'm not real, can't tell if words
can reach the dead. You'd know; you're
the one that's talking, who caught
your own reflection in the photo,
the image of an image through the glass.

2.

He's wrong. The long work of loss
doesn't happen in an instant.
It outlasts bodies, even memory.
The volcano on the horizon is still there.
Forget us or don't mourn us
and you won't suddenly be compassionate
for others on the newsreels.
We are them. Tomorrow, they'll be us.
Don't kid yourself. That's what
really kills us, the silt of apathy
and other men's concerns, softening
our outlines, year by year,
even me, who's still half sitting up,
trying for a last gasp of the air,
interrupting the smooth lines of the earth;
who'll never lie down.

Amanda Dalton

Lost Property

Racks of lost coats pushed together,
dreaming arms in their arms,
fingers buttoning, unbuttoning,
a warmth inside,

and boxes of umbrellas, upright, closed,
their nylon whispering at the rain
against the window, bent spokes straining
in a kind of reaching out.

A single leather gauntlet, still half-shaped
around the grip of handlebar,
still holding on, the roar and rush of air
against its back.

At his desk the clerk records the details
of discovery, attaches labels
to a broken doll, a brand new pair of shoes,
another coat, a hat.

He's sick of it, the stale smell of forgotten things,
the aftertaste of loss.
Beneath his desk he keeps old magazines:
Mayfair, Penthouse,

Annie, 23, from Stockholm
stares at him. He knows she's aching for it,
runs his finger down her body,
makes her wait.

Owen Sheers

The Swallows

The swallows are italic again,
cutting their sky-jive
between the telephone wires,
flying in crossed lines.

Their annual regeneration so flawless
to human eyes,
that there is no seam
between parent and child.

Just always the swallows
italic against the blue skies,
drink-dipping on the wing, wetting
the never-setting sun of their cut throats.

UNDERSTANDING

"Hello, 853009."

"Hello, Val? It's Meg. How are things? I promised I'd be in touch and here I am, true to my word."

"It's good to hear you. I'm not feeling too good at the moment, though; I'm so slow and stiff. My tablets wore off a bit too soon and I just can't get going. I'll be better in a while, once the tablets I've just taken kick in."

"Sorry to hear that. Tell me, I don't like to sound dumb, but although I know that Parkinson's makes people shake a lot, like my aunt did, - she couldn't stop, poor thing, - you didn't seem to be shaking at all when I saw you. So, what's Parkinson's Disease really like? You looked alright to me."

"Thank goodness for that. If I looked like I felt at times, I wouldn't go out. No two days are the same. I'm not an expert, but I have found out a lot about the condition. If you really want to find out the details it is best to get a book about it written by a qualified person, someone who has a thorough knowledge of the complaint.
Firstly, it isn't really a disease at all, and gradually the name is being shortened to one word: Parkinson's. If you have it, you are described as a person with Parkinson's. As I understand it, it is caused by a shortage of dopamine, a chemical needed in the part of the brain which controls movement."

"A chemical? Surely there's a cure for it in this day and age. They can do marvellous things now. New techniques are being discovered all the time for all sorts of complaints."

"You're right. But, no, there isn't a cure yet. There is a lot of research going on, though, and there are some fine doctors around. I'm lucky to have a very good consultant neurologist who has a very keen interest in the complaint, and a Parkinson's Specialist Nurse who works with him. Over the years they have become as friends, and if I feel worried about anything, I can ring and they are there to help. I go to the hospital to see the consultant once or twice a year, more often if I need to; he then reviews my condition, decides whether to amend my medication, writes to my GP with his report and recommendations and I am given a prescription every month. Works quite simply!"

"That's nice to know. The medical world takes a lot of criticism. But speak as you find, you seem to have been lucky, haven't you?"

"Oh, I have, indeed. Parkinson's is a progressive illness; it's here to stay so I may as well learn to put up with it. Actions that most people take for granted, such as walking, washing, bathing, getting out of bed, cleaning teeth, cooking, writing, shopping, socialising, even speaking, are difficult, and, at times, impossible. I could go on and on with the list."

"That's enough, isn't it? I never realised! But how do you get it? Is it catching?"

"No. Apparently, it isn't contagious and it isn't inherited - although there are incidences of it within families. In fact, I know a brother and sister who have it. It will not kill you and thankfully, there are tablets that help to ease the problems. I take medication in tablet form. There is no set drug regimen for all, but it has to be tailor made to suit. It's often a process of elimination, trying out various drugs before the doctor decides on the most suitable.

When the drugs are working, they reduce the symptoms so that you feel much better. Before the drugs kick in, or if they wear off before the next dose is due, things are not easy, and movement is difficult. That's what I'm like now. I can barely move."

"What are the symptoms, then?"

"Well, not everyone who has Parkinson's necessarily displays all or even the same symptoms. Each person is different. One of the main indicators of Parkinson's is rigidity and stiffness. The muscles are in a state of contraction, as tight as a drum. The body becomes rigid, the arms often don't swing when walking and the face becomes stiff and mask-like. It can affect you in so many ways, even speech. Have you noticed my speech? It's not easy to understand me, is it? Be honest. Talking is hard work for me."

"I must confess I have noticed a great change, at times it is extremely difficult to catch what you're saying, but I didn't like to mention it."

"At times, I can barely get a word out. My speech changes throughout the day; it's so frustrating and inhibiting. Sometimes I can speak fairly well. At times I can't get speech started, sometimes I freeze mid sentence. I'm often slow responding to questions and speech is often a monotone with no volume control. Some people become very impatient with me; it's very embarrassing. I also dribble a lot."

"I never realised Parkinson's was so bad."

"Another indicator of Parkinson's is slowness; it takes much longer to do things and to move about. Simple jobs prove difficult. It takes ages for me to get dressed in the morning - particularly putting on my tights and trousers.

Cleaning my teeth is impossible unless I use an electric toothbrush. Hoovering the floor is done in slow motion, and putting the duvet cover on is a nightmare. It's impossible to rush. Eating, especially in restaurants, is sometimes embarrassing because cutting food isn't easy and keeping the food on the fork and getting it into my mouth is a real test. I frequently need help to cut up my food."

" I would never have imagined it possible; you, needing help to eat."

"Turning over in bed at night is often impossible; my husband has to turn me over. I disturb him frequently at night. I sometimes need to go the bathroom and he has to ensure that I'm OK. I've lost my balance and fallen several times."

"What does Parkinson's feel like?"

"The best way I can describe what it feels like to have Parkinson's is for you to imagine you are wading through deep water; the weight of the water is so heavy and prevents you moving at speed, every movement is an effort as you have to push harder and harder to make progress. Nothing is easy."

"You must have found that hard to cope with. I remember you as being one of the most energetic women I knew; you'd have six or seven irons in the fire at one go. You were never idle. You always made me feel tired by just looking at you."

"Those days are long gone. Now, nothing is spontaneous, all tasks have to be thought out. I almost have to talk my way through jobs. Ironing shirts now takes me 15 minutes each shirt, instead of three in the same time. And the standard of ironing leaves much to be desired."

"You'll have to get him to iron his own shirts!"

"That'll be the day! But he has to do lots of things for me, such as handling heavy and hot cooking pans. He usually does things like that in case I drop them and scald myself. To get back to what we were talking about. You said your aunty shook. That shaking is known as tremor. Fortunately, I don't have that. The hands and feet shake rhythmically and uncontrollably when doing nothing and at rest. The muscles alternately contracting and relaxing at a rapid rate cause it. It must be awful, and it's so noticeable."

"My aunty used to get so embarrassed by it."

"I can understand why. There are other problems, too. There are changes in posture; walking becomes more of a shuffle, with a loss of balance causing stumbling and falls. I am usually covered in bruises; I fall over so easily.

22

Handwriting often becomes illegible and speech is affected in many people, as I've mentioned. Going shopping is a nightmare for me. I can't manipulate things easily, I can't pack the goods, somebody has to help. And I'm so clumsy; it's difficult to avoid bumping into people, I can't turn out of their way quickly enough. I need someone with me to manoeuvre the trolley. Handling money in my purse isn't easy. I can't write, so paying by cheque isn't possible, and when using a credit card, my signature is often challenged. I then get stressed and my speech becomes completely incoherent, causing me to panic."

"How do you manage buying clothes? You were always so well dressed?"

"The pleasure I had in clothes at one time has gone because I can't manage alone. I can't wander round the shops as easily as I could; I haven't the energy and I tend to panic in crowds, wandering about as though in a trance. Trying on clothes in changing rooms is extremely difficult; I get stuck and fail in mid-change and have to call for help which is very humiliating. Doing up buttons is often impossible. I tend to buy clothes in shops that will agree to take them back if unsuitable. It's surprising how many stores will allow this. I can try them on at home, taking my time. It's much easier."

"Tell me, how can doctors tell that it is Parkinson's?"

"It's not straightforward. There's no blood test, x-ray, or anything like that to definitely confirm Parkinson's. If there's a positive response to drug medication, Parkinson's can almost certainly be regarded as the problem."

"And drugs worked for you?"

"Oh, yes. Without my drugs I'd be lost. I have to take them at regular intervals throughout the day. If I forget, I'm soon in trouble. I take one called Sinemet. It contains a substance called L-dopa, and when it reaches the brain it changes into dopamine, the missing chemical. It's a form of replacement therapy. The other tablet I take is called Pergolide. This doesn't provide extra dopamine, but stimulates the brain to produce it. There are different strengths so the medication can be adjusted when necessary."

"Are they always effective?"

"Some days I'm better than other days, even though I take the same tablets. They sometimes take a long time to work in the morning, and sometimes they seem to 'run out of steam' before the next dose is due. It can be very awkward if the medication runs out while shopping; I've experienced this several times."

"That must be very distressing. Do many people have Parkinson's?"

23

"I've read that there are about one hundred and twenty thousand people with Parkinson's in the UK today. In every thousand people about fifteen have it. Most of these are elderly, but apparently, one in seven of those diagnosed is below fifty. I was 46. I've also read that some really young people have it. It must be hard for those with families if they have to give up work. I had to give up working, as you know. I taught for as long as I possibly could and I was reluctant to finish. I loved my job and it took a long time for me to come to terms with not teaching, but I couldn't write, my speech was extremely poor, both vital in teaching, so I didn't really have a choice, I'm sorry to say."

"You seem to be having difficulty speaking now. I'm finding it difficult to understand you. Perhaps you're getting tired. Anyway, I'd better ring off now, the family are coming for a meal tonight, so I'd better get cracking."

"Lovely to be in touch. I'll give you a call when I'm having a good speech day. Hang on; I've had an idea. Do you have e-mail? It's easier for me than phoning. There are times when I cannot even answer the phone."

"I've never used it. The whole idea frightens me stiff. I haven't learned how to use the video recorder yet, leave alone the computer."

"I couldn't manage without it now. It's become my lifeline. If I can manage it, anybody can. Two years ago I went on a course in the local college, one afternoon a week for three terms, and I learned word processing skills, spreadsheets and a lot more. I thoroughly enjoyed it; you ought to try it yourself. Any person who, like me, can't write would find it worthwhile."

"You are keen! I'll ask my grandson to show me how to send e-mails. He's just eight and in to 'IT' in a big way; and I'll certainly look into the possibility of classes for word processing."

"Times are certainly changing; we can't sit and watch but we have to move on, too. Send me your e-mail address and I'll mail you; that will give you the incentive to learn. You'll enjoy it eventually."

"OK. I'll have a go. Bye for now."

Christopher Meredith

Message

…no secrets which appeared to require concealment were revealed.
  Anthony Storr, *Solitude*

She hid her notebooks underneath a board.
All her secret years were what she'd written
And the message - oh the message was in code.

The Lonely Child, Creative, Bright, Ignored
Kept diaries according to the pattern
And hid her notebooks underneath a board.

Years later, experts come upon the hoard
- Keys to the great writer's motivation
But the message, ah, the message is in code.

They clap their hands. So much to be explored
Deciphering the secret heart of a woman
Who hid her notebooks underneath a board.

And that unlocking lets light on what's stored -
Eventless commonplaces. An empty room. The burden
Is no message is the message in the code.

She knows the cipher's greater than the word.
What's on display's the fact that all is hidden
So she hides her notebooks underneath a board
And the message is the message is in code.

Robert Minhinnick

Samphire

After the hurricane blew
Through my head I knew

Things had to change. That silence
Was no longer a defence.

So walking on the eastern shore
I asked myself what I was for,

And on that beach I built a fire
For the pickers of samphire,

Their plasticbags and fingers thick
With the samphire's citric

Oils, our thoughts turning to supper
Of seabass, or a silver -

Side of sewin laid
In tinfoil in the pit I'd made

On a griddle over ingots
Of driftwood, white-hot

In seconds, the firestones black
With armfuls of the bladderwrack

Like strings of jalapenos spread
To dry, so that the fire spat

Purple as tramsparks, its smoke a sail
To the northeast, and as night fell

We saw spectres in that auditorium,
Our shadows in the salty flame -

Giants as the blaze grew higher
Crowned with pluckings of samphire -

And then behind us on the dune
Another light appeared, and soon

Another, further up the bay,
And voices if we listened carefully,

Some soft, some crazed
In the darkness where the fires blazed.

White lightning drinkers
Under the flickering meniscus

Of the dogstar, and speedfreaks'
Midnight histrionics,

Mad as sandfleas round the beacon
On the summit of Tom Brython,

Ambassadors of turbulence
Whose private language yet made sense,

Then deep in the dewpits of the warren
The nightjar's prothalamium

To a new moon: true voices all
In the dark's confessional,

Admitting the imperative
That how we speak is how we live.

And even our deliriums
Are more than debris of our dreams.

So when I heard the hurricane
I guessed it might not come again,

But what it offers is the choice
To use, or not, a tiny voice

And watch it flaring like a spark
In duneland's neolithic dark.

And maybe the next morning find
The fire has left a frost behind.

Roger McGough

The Railings

You came to watch me playing cricket once,
Quite a few of the fathers did.
At ease, outside the pavilion
they would while away a Saturday afternoon.
Joke with the masters, urge on
their flannelled offspring. But not you.

Fielding deep near the boundary
I saw you through the railings.
You were embarrassed when I waved
and moved out of sight down the road.
When it was my turn to bowl though
I knew you'd still be watching.

Third ball, a wicket, and three more followed.
When we came in at the end of the innings
the other dads applauded and joined us for tea.
Of course, you had gone by then. Later,
you said you'd found yourself there by accident.
Just passing. Spotted me through the railings.

       *   *   *   *   *

Speech days: Prize–givings: School-plays
The Twentyfirst: The Wedding: The Christening
You would find yourself there by accident.
Just passing. Spotted me through the railings.

29

Michael Donaghy

The New Grey

It's black, it says here, but not jet, not shiny,
more the charcoal black old family snapshots burn,
the dark of the cathedral vault aswarm with pigeons
muted to an expensive almost-blue-black.
See a woman in black? See me touching her shoulder?
We weren't friends, but…What? Hear my words
blow out like lamps in series down a mine shaft?
The colour of the coal dust rising up to gag me
is this new shade, exactly. Can we discuss this?
I need to get fluent in grey if I want to survive.
I need a job to earn enough to buy that shirt
in the same unsayable black that hid in the wardrobe
in a room I woke in as a child.

CONTEMPLATION

E-mail to: <u>val@linkusup.fun</u>

Dear Val

    This is my first attempt at e-mail. Hope you receive it. Send one to me to confirm. Tell me, how long were you able to work? Why did you eventually give up?

Best wishes,

Meg

E-mail to: <u>meg@beamsaway.con</u>

Hi, Meg

    It was good to receive your mail.
    Things gradually worsened. At times I felt really bad, afraid to be seen in company because I couldn't guarantee how I'd be. My speech was poor, I had no stamina, and I was suffering side effects from my medication. My body would go into a state of uncontrollable writhing – dreadful and exhausting. When in school, I'd try to disguise it by wrapping my legs around the legs of the chair, and folding my arms tight to my chest to restrain myself.
    Rarely went to the Staff Room - became something of an isolate. Felt so lonely and humiliated. To see the embarrassment on colleagues' faces when they noticed my strange movements was hard to bear. It was easier to remain apart as often as I could. Being apart from people, spending my time in my own room gave me a lot of time to think and made me aware of the concept of time and how we don't make the best use of it when we can.
    Time on your hands, and a complaint, which is with you to stay, has a tendency of making one introspective. I felt that I had to be positive and do my best to stay strong. Giving in and feeling sorry for oneself is the easiest thing in the world. People have enough problems of their own and are not really interested in being an Agony Aunt. They will do their best to avoid you if you become a moaner.

Best wishes

Val

E-mail to: val@linkusup.fun

Dear Val,

Thanks for your reply. I've been practising. My grandchildren can't get a look in now! I do feel a rotter!

Met Beryl King on Tuesday. Her sister, Bronwen, in college with you, has just been diagnosed with Parkinson's. What a coincidence! She's very depressed. I can understand that. Certain I would be, too. Were you?

Meg

E-mail to: meg@beamsaway.con

Dear Meg,

Sorry to hear about Beryl's sister. I'll write to her. I've got her address somewhere. Haven't seen her in years.

Yes, I felt down, and have had negative feelings, but I'm lucky to be very strong willed and determined. Can hide my feelings, put a front on. Proud, too. Didn't want people's sympathy. Became more aware of people about me. I was being observed just as I enjoy watching others.

My feelings change from time to time. Sometimes I worry about how bad I'm going to get and how I'll manage if left alone. I suppose I'm strong only because I have my family about me. If I were totally alone, I may not be so positive. Other times my concern is for my family. I feel angry that at some time they'll be burdened with me.

Val

E-mail to: val@linkusup.fun

Dear Val,

I'm taking my mother back home on Saturday. She's much better now and anxious to be in her own place again.

I'll call in to see you on Sunday morning before I return home, if it's OK with you.

Meg

John Burnside

For Sarah

I used to think old age would be like this:
the afternoons more sudden than they are
in childhood, and the snow against the glass

more final, like the sports-announcer's voice
reading the football results while our neighbours' lights
quickened against the blackness out of doors.

I was seven, or seventeen, and I didn't know
how ageing works, like Zeno's paradox,
adjusting all the time, to right itself;

yet sometimes, on a winter's afternoon,
I thought of someone skilled – a juggler, say –
adjusting to the pull of gravity

by shifts and starts, till something in the flesh
- a weightedness, a plumb-line to the earth –
revealed itself, consenting to be still.

Anne Stevenson

Washing my Hair

Contending against a restless shower head,
    I lather my own.
The hot tap, without a mind, decides
    to scald me;
The cold, without a will, would rather
    freeze me.
Tuning them to suit me is an act of flesh
    I know as mine.
Here am I: scalp, neck, back, breasts,
    armpits, spine,
Parts I've long been part of, yet never
    treasured much,
Since I absorb them not *by* touch, more
    because of touch.
It's my mind, I think, with its hoard of horribles,
    That's 'me'.
Or is it really? I fantasize it bodiless,
    set free:
No bones, no skin, no hair, no nerves,
    just memory,
Untouchable, unwashable, and not, I guess,
    my own.
Still, none will know me better when I'm
    words of stone
Than I, these creased familiar hands
    and clumsy feet.
My soul, how will I recognise you
    if we meet?

Helen Dunmore

Depot

The panting of buses through caves of memory:
school bus with boys tossing off
in the back seat when I was eight,
knowing the words, not knowing
what it was those big boys were murkily doing,
and the conductor with fierce face
yelling down farm lanes at kids as they ran
Can you not get yourselves up in the morning?

The sway of buses into town,
the way the unlopped branches of lime
knocked like sticks against railings,
the way women settled laps and bags,
shut their eyes, breathed out on a fag,
gave themselves to nothing for ten minutes
as someone else drove the cargo of life,
until the conductor broke their drowse
in a flurry of one-liners
and they found coin in their fat purses.

Stephen Knight

Some Other Forms of Modern Treatment

(for my father)

We need a cure for snow:
a level tablespoon,
one jab to make the winter go.
We need a panacea soon
- something for pain -

perhaps a doctor to explain
low cloud away,
a tonic for the rain
washing over Langland Bay,
an ointment to apply to fog,

inhalers, creams, blue pills
to combat hail and sleet
or medicine that kills
black ice on every street;
something painless, please,

something strong to ease
the squalls, to calm
the shaking of the trees
- their naked arms,
their hollowed hearts.

Gwyneth Lewis

Spit it Out

Their love couldn't save her, it was the knock
as they dropped the glass coffin. The shock

dislodged the apple in Snow White's throat,
made her start coughing. "Spit it out!"

encouraged Grumpy. Dock fussed, "Stand back,
I'm trained for this." As Snow White choked

on the poison she'd swallowed, facing death,
his Heimlich manoeuvre jolted her breath

and the purging started. First, a violent hack
sprayed out spittle, so the crowd stood back,

but a glob of the apple had shot out hard,
covered in mucous, lodged in Sleepy's beard,

where it dripped on his trousers. The company gasped
at the hosings of acid waterbrash,

then projectile vomit, a terrible black,
as her tiny frame tried to clear the block

in her oesophagus. Bashful caught her teeth
in a porcelain bowl he held underneath

her working gullet. Next came some words
in a private language that sounded weird

and then the objects for which they stood:
six saucepans, a tea set, then firewood,

a ball-cock, some money, a broken syringe,
twelve roughly hewn boulders from an unfinished henge

(they came out in hiccups), rusty nails,
two miles of barbed wire looped in bales,

then the artillery, booming out shells,
a Panzer division form her personal hell,

then a Red Cross unit. All round her fumes
from her inner corruption made everyone swoon -

rotten seagulls' eggs with a hint of skunk,
And then her waters or, rather, her gunk

broke and she turned herself inside out
neatly, a clutch bag through her own throat,

her lungs a silk lining. Her tiny voice changed
to a contralto as her jaws' hinge

gaped and she found behind her lics
what she'd meant all along, not the alibis

she'd created with sweetness. The witch's curse
was shed now so, like an emptied purse

she took herself back again with a gulp,
began to feel hungry. In a pool of gloop

the dwarves stood, dripping with day-glo snot.
"Did I say something wrong, boys? What is it? *What?*"

OPTIMISM

"Oh! Hello, Meg. I thought I heard the doorbell! I was in the kitchen. Do come in."

"Good to see you again, Val. I've brought Beryl with me."

"How good to see you both. Haven't seen you for a long time, Beryl. I was really sorry to hear that your sister has Parkinson's. How is she? I wrote to her only yesterday; she'll probably have my letter tomorrow."

"Nice to see you, too. Thanks for writing to her; she'll be pleased to hear from you. I'm very worried about her and I feel so helpless. I don't know anything about the complaint. She is finding it very hard coming to terms with it."

"That's natural; it takes time for it to sink in. Some people won't accept the diagnosis and live in a state of denial for some time; I have a friend who is reluctant to take her medication. Many are positively frightened; others read as much as they can about it, including medical textbooks, becoming obsessed with the epidemiology. Some isolate themselves, through embarrassment, while others feel sorry for themselves and become totally dependent on their wife or husband to do things they are not yet incapable of doing for themselves. I've probably been through all of these stages in turn."

"Bronwen has changed such a lot, both physically and emotionally. Is this normal? Has your condition changed much over the years? Are you getting worse?"

"It is a progressive complaint, and, yes, I feel it is worsening. At best, helped by the drugs it is 'on hold'. It got to a stage for about a year before I finished school that I was suffering not only with the symptoms of Parkinson's but also from severe side effects from my drugs. I think I've already mentioned these side effects to you, Meg, haven't I?"

"As if it isn't bad enough. What are they like?"

"There are various side effects which may be experienced by some: nausea and sickness, depression, hallucinations, cramps. The side effect that gave me most trouble was something called dyskinesia. My body would become crazy; uncontrollable movements ranging from barely noticeable twitches and jerks to dreadful twisting and writhing movements, involving any part of the body, occurred several times a day. Nothing could be done to stop them; they would last for periods of an hour or so, easing gradually before coming to an end, leaving me utterly exhausted."

"What caused it?"

"Apparently it's caused by an overdose of dopamine, the chemical I told you about, Meg. Sometimes the brain becomes hypersensitive to it, or, you may become resistant to Sinemet, the medication containing L-dopa, and need higher doses of the drug to control your symptoms. In either case the brain receives more dopamine than it can handle at certain points of the day. I used to have these attacks in school, which was difficult, and in the evenings at home."

"Do you still have these dys... dys..?"

"Dyskinesia. Yes, at times, but much reduced, thanks to an operation in February 1996. I was lucky to be able have brain surgery."

"An operation? I thought you said Parkinson's has no cure."

"That's true, Meg, but advances have been made to help reduce the dreadful symptoms. There are different types of operation depending on the symptoms. What I had is called a pallidotomy. The hospital consultant referred me to a neurosurgeon in another hospital. I had the operation in February 1996, and the results were instantaneous. The embarrassing, horrific writhing stopped. It was a blessed relief. The operation was performed while I was fully conscious, and I can honestly say that it was the most exciting and exhilarating experience of my life, one that I will never forget. I still need to take medication, - the complaint won't go away - but the problem of writhing has certainly been reduced."

"Conscious? Ugh! Was it dreadfully painful?"

"Not at all. Apparently, the brain itself is not able to feel pain. I can reassure anyone who needs such an operation. There is nothing to fear of the operation in itself: although, obviously, no surgery of any type is risk free. There are great advances being made in Parkinson's research, and there is so much to be optimistic about. There are various things being developed, too technical for me to understand so I won't even try to talk about it, but I'm sure that there will be a cure one day; maybe not for me, but perhaps for the next generation."

41

Jo Shapcott

Gwaithla Garden

after Rilke

It's like you to spot
the small butterfly near the ground
showing off the illustrations
in its flying manual

and to describe it like that, and the other one
closing in on the edge of the flower
we're all breathing now because
you wrote it in 1922 and , O

beloved, this is not the moment to read you
into it, but to see the fragile blues
scattered, floating and flying
like the blue upstrokes and downstrokes

of this torn-up love letter in the wind
I've been writing you for ages
while the postman
hovered for it at the door.

Peter Finch

Paint

Violent White
Azure Eyepatch
Winter Arse
Gurgling Sands
Underarm Crush
Blueberry Sandinista
Tropical Testosterone
Sunkist Yellow Underpant
Vanilla Vertigo
Mango Virginia
Warm Topsoil
Duodenum Jade
Fresh Acne

What is the maximum number of times
you have to repaint the
wall below the dado?

Seven.

Leslie Norris

Black Currants, Red Currants

He sits with his mother
on a low wall near the grass.
She is preparing garden fruit,
black currants, red currants,
for a summer pudding.

The child's eyes are closed.
He can feel inside his head
the tart smell of currants.
His aunt is talking to his mother.
He does not know he is listening.

"He's only two," she says,
"It breaks my heart
to hear him call for her."
"When's the funeral?" his mother says;
his aunt, "Tomorrow, tomorrow afternoon."

His cousin Bobby, a baby
scarcely able to stagger,
sits in the dust, gurgling,
following with his finger
a straggling insect.

Each morning the boy's mother
touches his throat. She is afraid
he will catch diphtheria
like other children in the town.
He is not afraid. With Edgar Carey

he has run the whole length
of the Fever Hospital wall,
running hard, his mouth closed,
holding his breath all the way,
and is proof against contagion.

He does not know
he will stand in his garden,
stained by his own harvest,
roses open in the sun,
tomatoes warm on the vine,

yellow peaches ripening,
listening to the motherless child
calling over years and countries,
"I'm here, Mummy! Mummy, I'm here!"
But the mother is dead, and dead

the brown-haired baby,
toddling Bobby Norris,
for all that careful lifting
from the dirt, for all the prayers.
Before he had run a step.

Paul Muldoon

Hard Drive

With my back to the wall
and a foot in the door
and my shoulder to the wheel
I would drive through Seskinore.

With an ear to the ground
and my neck on the block
I would tend to my wound
in Belleek and Bellanaleck.

With a toe in the water
and a nose for trouble
and an eye to the future
I would drive through Derryfubble

and Dunnamanagh and Ballynascreen,
keeping that wound green.

Andrew Motion

Buddleia

Travelling by various ingenious routes,
sometimes in the cargo-hold of a swallow,
at others bedded on the lint of a coat pocket,

or struck in the sole of a seasoned traveller,
buddleia has worked its way into this tight
corner of my garden. There is no way

it can speak a word in my own language,
but this does not matter a damn to me.
I have already learned how to cherish

its different ways of getting in touch,
which range from a hard scratching
through to hushed water-murmurs.

Most of all I love the beauty
in its straight-up flower-prongs:
tongues to some, but in truth more

like a chemical fire the very second
it flares and takes hold. Flame-jets
at once solid and see-through,

a gust of heat, and the certain idea
that what has started now cannot stop
except when it lies low, and then re-kindles.

Lynne Rees

In Praise of Things

Today I want to say something wonderful
about my potato peeler -
the way the ergonomically designed handle
fits snugly in the curve of my palm as if
it was made for the valley of my right hand.

I want to tell you how it is soul-mate
to thick-skinned vegetables –
cloudy tangerine columns of carrot,
knobbly orbs of King Edward.
How it slides over them as if it might be
wrapping not unwrapping them
as if it might be whispering
while secretly stealing their skin.

I love the way the steel head swivels
gently rocking from side to side
accommodating each slight ridge
bump lesion. Under the skin

everything glistens new born -
vulnerable exposed true colours rising.

ACCEPTANCE

"You were lucky, weren't you? Couldn't you have gone back to school after the operation?"

"I would have liked to, but there were other problems which made teaching impossible. I can't write at all. My handwriting is undecipherable, getting smaller and smaller until it's a straight line - known as micrographia. I depend on my computer for letters, but I have to ask others to complete forms for me. And as you have noticed, my speech is very poor, at times it is totally incoherent and it is causing me to be very depressed. I don't know whether my speech problem is a result of the operation or perhaps it would have been just the same anyway. It wasn't good before the operation. If you can't write or speak, then teaching is one job which is impossible."

"Have you ever felt bitter about the fact that you have got this complaint? I'm sure I would."

"No, I can honestly say that I haven't felt bitter. I'm fortunate that I accept that life is "Que Sera, Sera". What's to be will be. I've always accepted that there is no point in worrying about things that are unable to be changed. I would be lying if I said that I never feel low, but my depression doesn't last long, and I continue to look on the bright side. What is fact, is that I am not as bad as many Parkinson patients, and there are lots of illnesses that cause pain and discomfort."

"How do you fill your time? You've always been so occupied. You've worked all your adult life, haven't you?"

"Yes, I had six months off when my daughter was born but I've worked ever since. I had clocked up 32 years teaching by the time I retired, 22 of those in my last school, doing a job I loved. I was always busy at home, too; doing housework, playing the piano, sewing, embroidering, knitting; I had two large dogs needing exercise each day, so I was never idle. I didn't go out socially very often, I didn't feel the need, or have the desire to. My husband had a very time-demanding job and I didn't have pleasure in going places without him.

Now, though, if I'm honest, I wish I had been more sociable. Perhaps I'd have more to do, more places to visit with friends. But one loses the art of socialising and the way I am now, makes it more difficult. I've lost my confidence and my self-esteem. I try not to compare myself with one or two people I know who have good health, are outgoing, have their company sought after and are enjoying the kind of life style I thought I would be enjoying in middle age; but, I must confess, there are times when I feel inferior and threatened."

"I can't believe it! You used to be so confident; you were always in control, always the leader. Never afraid to talk or perform at the piano in public. You were such an accomplished pianist, and now you say you can't play. What a loss!"

"I'm unable to move my fingers quickly enough and get the timing right. My singing voice, once extremely good has become a screech, and I can't teach piano privately because of my speech. I've lost confidence because I can't guarantee how I'm going to be."

"Why is it that sometimes you are better than others?"

"There are times when the symptoms are more severe and certain activities are not possible - these are known as 'off' periods. During 'on' periods I can cope reasonably well. The trouble is that these good and bad times are so unpredictable. The differences may be due to the Parkinson's itself or may be drug induced. One-minute things are great, and the next, almost like flicking the light switch, immobility has set in and I can hardly move."

"How awful!"

"People don't always understand, and can mistake your slowness and detachment for indifference and laziness."

"How do you manage if you are alone?"

'Going 'off' when out is very awkward. This is why I don't go far from home on my own. I've been in Tesco's, gone 'off', and have had to sit down for half hour or so while my tablet kicks in, because it is literally impossible to carry on; reaching the car is a giant feat.
Another embarrassing aspect of Parkinson's for me is that at times I appear drunk. I can't control my head, it moves from side to side, and with my poor speech, one can't blame people for thinking that I've been hitting the bottle. I dislike answering the phone because I simply can't feel sure that my mouth will utter what my mind is thinking.
Still, that's life, I suppose. What we can't change, there's no other option than to accept."

Dannie Abse

The Abandoned

There is no space unoccupied by the Shekinah- Talmud

*…thy absence doth excel
All distance known* – George Herbert

1. God, when you came to our house
    we let you in. Hunted,
    we gave you succour,
    bandaged your hands,
    bathed your feet.

Wanting water we gave you wine.
Wanting bread we gave you meat.

Sometimes, God, you should recall
we are your hiding-place.
Take away these hands
and you would fall.

Outside, the afflicted pass.
We only have to call.
They would open you
with crutch and glass.

Who else then could we betray
if not you, the nearest?
God, how you watch us
and shrink away.

2. Never have we known you so transparent.
   You stand against the curtain and wear
   its exact design. And if a window opens
   (like a sign) then is it you
   or the colours that are blown apart?

   You startle from room to room, apologising.

   God, you can't help your presence
   any more than the glassy air that lies
   between tree and skies. No need to pass
   through wave-lengths human ears can't sense.

   We never hear the front door close when you are leaving.
   Sometimes we question if you are there at all.
   No need to be so self-effacing;
   quiet as language of the roses
   or moss upon the wall.

   We have to hold our breath to hear you breathing.

3. Dear God in the end you had to go.
   Dismissing you, your absence made us sane.
   We keep the bread and wine for show.

   The white horse galloped across the snow,
   melted, leaving no hoof marks in the rain.
   Dear God, in the end you had to go.

   The winds of war and derelictions blow,
   howling across the radioactive plain.
   We keep the bread and wine for show.

Sometimes what we do not know we know –
who can count the stars, call each one by name?
Dear God in the end you had to go.

Yet boarding the last ship out all sorrow
that grape is but grape and grain is grain.
We keep the bread and wine for show.

Soon night will be like feathers of the crow,
small lights upon the shore begin to wane.
Dear God in the end you had to go,
we keep the bread and wine for show.

4. Now, God, you are the colour black.
   Who prays, 'Come down, Thou, come down?'
   Absurd saints search for the rack.
   Omnipotence is what you lack
   even when you stumble back.

   Did you weep when you found us out?
   Did you return to blaspheme
   cursing Man? (Then should we be devout?)
   Already you begin to doubt
   if you really heard us shout.

   Was it your own voice, God, that cried?
   Sulky, you thrust back the bolt
   against the human noise outside.
   Oh open the damned door wide.
   Maybe someone dear has died.

   Listen. Can't you hear again
   an idiot desperate in a house,
   the strict economy of pain,
   a voice pleading and profane
   calling you by name?

Carole Bromley

Thomas

By the simple act of leaning
from my arm, he makes me
disappear. And reappear at will,
and disappear again.

I watch his surprise,
an idea dawning, that chuckle.
Today he's a god,
where he goes I go too.

Later he'll bang a fist
on his reflection, eat his face
in a spoon and stand alone,
wondering who he is.

Bernard O'Donaghue

Chough

Old redfoot-jackdaw, you know where
to pick your retirement home, drawn
to the southern sweep of the Great Blasket
where Europe's tourists, all got up
in Aran ganseys, cower against
the August squall. When the rain stops
they'll hear you, cryking behind them
somewhere off the moss-soft beaten track;
or, when the sun's come out again,
outside the clubhouse in Ballybunion
where you while away the summer afternoon
in the company of other withdrawing exiles.
What taxman could make you out down there?

Theodore Weiss

Command Performance

As capable a troupe of super
stars as we could hope for.
But which one, having dressed
in hand-me-downs out of a skimpy
wardrobe, is acting up?
                          However
each exhorts us, we can hardly
tell them apart. Is this what
ensemble playing means?
                          But now
a grizzled king, tricked out
in assorted stinking body rags,
lurched roaring
                          across the boards,
wields a dagger athirst for blood,
the rest of the cast swept along,
subject to his madness.
                          And we,
less than captivated, yet a captive
audience, also play our bit part --
clobbered zany, butt, whatever --
in this command performance.

If only, our cast ever rehearsing
their roles on us, we could find
it in ourselves to appreciate
their art, their ardencies!

Val Bowden

Letter to Bronwen

I've recently heard that you've been diagnosed with Parkinson's, I am so sorry. I'd like to meet up with you so we can chat; the main thing is that you don't worry. I hope that this letter will help you to see that although life will change, you can cope. You simply must take the most positive view, never lose faith; don't mope. To explain what it's like to have Parkinson's is not easy as I'm sure you'll believe. Each day is a challenge, simple tasks are often so hard to achieve. One day I feel almost as normal as before I had PD, then the next I'm fidgeting, writhing and stammering; it's taken its toll on me.

But thankfully, reasoning remains intact; my mind's not affected at all. It has its ability, the same as before PD took hold; but life's no ball! My body has changed, responses have slowed, reactions take longer, that's true. Life isn't as easy or as secure, but at least I can cope; so will you. I can't easily plan to go out with a friend, as I can't say how long it will be before movement slows down and my strength disappears. This feeling is awful; believe me. One moment I look pretty normal and can join in the action with ease but the next I'm struck down, I'm unable to move, the body has gone into "freeze."

I try to look good, I like to dress well and when I am feeling 'A1', which isn't that often, I'm sorry to say, I enjoy a good laugh and some fun. Friends often remark that I look very well, but they see just the outer display, for reality's different, they don't know the truth: I avoid them on a bad day. I'm really quite lucky, not half as bad as many who have this complaint. I've not got the tremor, the incessant shaking; that's enough to tease even a saint. I'm able to do the most personal things

without help, so I don't feel the pain that many must feel when
they need to be cared for by others: that must be a strain.

The brain is the most precious part of our body, but
faults in it sometimes appear. In Parks, the main reason is
dopamine shortage, what causes this is not quite clear. Without
it the body refuses to move because muscles receive no
commands so tablets are taken to make up the losses: there are
so many different brands. To be controlled by the drugs that we
need is a bind. The timing is such that the day's medication is
taken with care, too little is wrong, and too much. But it would
be far worse if there were no relief; the alternative does not bear
thought. There'd be no life, no freedom from pain; the drugs
make one's life far less fraught. You'd think that drugs taken at
regular times should work predictably, but often they don't and
are slow to kick in, I find that a mystery. It's really a puzzle why
some days the body feels able to move without strain, while the
next it will either refuse to perform, - or refuse to keep still, - it's
a pain! When working their best the drugs bring relief; it's great
when the body's at peace. When fading one feels a significant
slowing, a lack of response - movements cease. Rigidity often
accompanies this "off", it's a stiffness I can't explain, and one
has to be patient and wait for what seems like a light being
switched on again.

But there are two sides to a coin: I've found the drugs
can have adverse effects. Too large a dose may cause shaking
and twisting and writhing. One has to expect this awful
experience to take its own course, it cannot be stopped at one's
will, but when it recedes, the feeling is such that you're thankful
the body's so still.

It's not easy to cope, knowing that I have changed into
someone who cannot control my mouth which now opens and

spills out saliva; nor the eyes, which continually roll. To feel that I should not converse - for the sounds that I utter will make me sound drunk – results in my not going out quite so often, instead living just like a monk. The feelings of humiliation occur, because I know that I often seem weak. It's hard to accept that the person I was has long ago passed her peak. It's hard to accept that as yet there's no cure, - but keep hope that in time there may be. It's not easy to realise there will come a time when I'll lose independency.

Most people with Parkinson's are reaching old age; they are OAP's and have retired. But many have been diagnosed when quite young; life for these has backfired. They have families, mortgages, debts to repay; they need to have jobs, they need cash. For some, work is possible, helped by the drugs, but for many, work ends with a crash.

Important to people with Parkinson's are the carers who readily give so much of their time, at hand to assist, making life so much easier to live. The carer's devotion and patience is needed, but they can become worn out by strain, giving up so much time, often losing their freedom for others, with nothing to gain. I'm not yet quite sixty, but for fourteen years I've had Parkinson's. It's here to stay, so there's no point in fighting, denying or hiding; it certainly won't go away. I take the advice of my doctor and the Parkinson's Specialist Nurse; and I try to be positive, meeting with others who share this atrocious curse.

It hasn't been long since you learned what you have. I urge you, have positive sights. Although life will change, you'll have to adapt; seek help and secure all your rights. I'm not an expert; I speak from the heart - I often feel frightened and sad - but fate can't be changed by self-pity and dread: count the good things in life, not the bad.

Matthew Francis

Christmas Walk

We spread out over the slope
and made for the white sky,
big and little, in hoods,
a pilgrimage in landscape.

The country's sunk in itself,
slimed with its winter fertility,
cabbage-scent, cottony hedge-growths,
fields of serious brown -

stop to tie your lace
and they don't want to let go,
glue you like one of those dreams.
You think you won't catch up,

that the big, little, hooded
figures beyond the brow
are already walking
down the slope of another year.

Paul Henry

The Short Cut to the Sea

No one's charted this way
except by heart. The bay
opens up at the end.

Already stitching the torn land
back to the dazzling sea
or bending to untie
the straps from your brown feet,
you've left me behind.

"Wait for me! Wait!"
cries the land to the sea.

Jeremy Hooker

Homer Dictating

for Gerard Casey

It is the body that speaks
and what it speaks of is the man
and his suffering, his thought,
the vision he sees in his blindness.

His hands speak,
and his mouth speaks more than words,
and his whole body,
an old man's but still powerful.

In the depths behind his eyes
warriors boast on the windy field,
Odysseus adventures on the seas,
among magical and dangerous islands,
and strains his eyes against the light
and sting of spray to catch a wisp of smoke
far off, rising from the hearth-fires of Ithaca.

Rembrandt's Homer is a man,
but the light of the sacred
is upon him -
a pale watery gold
falling across his shoulders and his face.
But it does not shine from afar,
from another world.
The sacred is part of him,
dwelling in light and shadow,
and his body is the landscape of his soul.

For the painter has taken clay in his hands,
common clay,
and shaped it from its image, God-given,
which he knew in his own world,
among merchants and soldiers,
Rabbis and adventurers,
the grand and poor of Leiden
and Amsterdam, and knew
most intimately in his own flesh,
in the imagination that is breath and blood and spirit.

With this he saw, and humbled his seeing
to know the vision of the blind,
of Homer dictating,
with sightless eyes,
the seer of men and women and gods.

Margaret Atwood

The Ottawa River By Night

In the full moon you dream more.
I know where I am: the Ottawa River
far up, where the dam goes across.
Once, midstorm, in the wide cold water
upstream, two long canoes full
of children tipped, and they all held hands
and sang till the chill reached their hearts.
I suppose in our waking lives that's the best
we can hope for, if you think of that moment
stretched out for years.
                              Once, my father
and I paddled seven miles
along a lake near here
at night, with the trees like a pelt of dark
hackles, and the waves hardly moving.
In the moonlight the way ahead was clear
and obscure both. I was twenty
and impatient to get there, thinking
such a thing existed.

                        None of this
is in the dream, of course. Just the thick square-
edged shape of the dam, and eastward
the hills of sawdust from the mill, gleaming as white
as dunes. To the left, stillness; to the right,
the swirling foam of rapids
over sharp rocks and snags; and below that, my father,
moving away downstream
in his boat, so skilfully
although dead, I remember now; but no longer as old.
He wears his grey hat, and evidently
he can see again. There now,
he's around the corner. He's heading eventually
to the sea. Not the real one, with its sick whales
and oil slicks, but the other sea, where there can still be
safe arrivals.
                        Only a dream, I think, waking
to the sound of nothing.
Not nothing. I heard: it was a beach, or shore,
and someone far off, walking.
Nowhere familiar. Somewhere I've been before.
It always takes a long time
to decipher where you are.

Tony Curtis

Eggs

How your childhood is pieced together.
This Christmas he tells you about
your grandfather
out at night with three caps –
one for his head against the weather,
and one slipped over each boot,
so that he left no print in the snow
across the farmyard to the chickens.
As quiet as snow itself,
under the cracked moon
his hands slipping softly
into the warm, drowsy nests.
And the polished ochre eggs bursting
their bright suns in the morning pan,
one secret and one secret and another.

Tony Curtis

La Cathédrale Engloutie

i.m. Ceri Richards

The drowned bells keen for the sinner and the knave,
between felled pillars and glass the damned swim free –
light and music still play beneath the waves.

The ocean breathes and stretches through caves
so rowdy gulls rise to slice the sky. They flee
the drowned bells, keen for sinners and knaves.

For the dry world above is ruled by power-slaves
who are deaf to deep truths, can't see
light and music still plays beneath the waves

that circle and define the land: we must learn to love
and live by old rhythms, each fold of the sea.
The drowned bells keen for the sinners and the knaves

as death claims the weak, the noble and the brave
in equal part. Time's indifferent to sacrifice or plea.
Light and music still play beneath the waves –

our vision and need, what each soul craves
is figured in our fallen churches, as Debussy knew, and Ceri.
The drowned bells keen for the sinners and the knaves,
light and music still play beneath the waves.

POSITIVE THINKING

"I've learned a lot today. I feel more able to help my sister now. But I feel sorry if you can't have any pleasure from physical activity. Being confined to the house is not pleasant, is it?"

"No, you're right, and people with Parkinson's shouldn't isolate themselves. I'm luckier than many, and when the drugs are on form, I make sure that I make the most of it. Two years ago, I went one day a week for 12 weeks, on a course in the hospital, organised by my consultant and the Parkinson's Specialist nurse. It was well run and it gave me a new vision and outlook on life. I believe such courses are run in other areas. Your sister should make enquiries to see if her hospital has something similar. It would be of tremendous help to her."

"Sounds interesting. What did it involve?"

"The course included physiotherapy; we were taught moving techniques and given exercises to improve our joints and muscles, our posture and our breathing. We had occupational therapy sessions where we learnt useful coping strategies to assist in daily life. A speech therapist provided help with the control of the voice and we had speakers on various interesting topics including a speaker who gave information concerning our eligibility for benefits."

"All worthwhile stuff."

"It certainly was. The importance of exercise was stressed and we had a circuit session each week. We were encouraged to be as active as possible, and not to assume that exercise was beyond us. It was great to meet with other people with Parkinson's; I made some new friendships there and all of us were sorry when it finished.

I decided after the course that I ought to continue with exercise and I joined an exercise class for people with health problems. There are people who have cardiac and back problems and the instructor is fully qualified."

"Is it helpful?"

"I enjoy it. It's only low impact level, nothing too ambitious. We have stretch and toning floor exercises, too. I just make sure that my drugs are at the optimum point for action and I do my best. Some days, my legs won't work and I have to leave or sit it out, but the people there understand. There is no embarrassment; every one is very friendly. It has social benefits as well as physical ones because I've made new friends, which is nice. I really look forward to these sessions."

"Do you go on your own?"

"No, my friend comes with me. She is so patient, never becoming irritated when I have difficulty moving or speaking. When people show their impatience it makes things worse. She waits patiently and doesn't try to hurry me or speak for me, but maintains her interest in what I'm trying to say."

"I'm surprised about the exercise class. I would have thought that exercise would be impossible."

"I'm seriously thinking of taking up yoga instead. A friend of mine who has Parkinson's goes to a low level class twice a week and she says that she has found it most helpful. Her body is less tense; she finds it easier to relax and her coordination has improved. Exercise is so important."

"You put me to shame. Is there an association for Parkinson's?"

"Yes, there is a Parkinson's Disease Society. I've been a member for some years. The society is very important, as it's able to help and support patients and relatives. There is a help line so, if in doubt or worried, help is only a phone call away. I don't go to many meetings, but I look forward to the quarterly magazine, with its interesting and informative articles. Probably, though, the society is most valuable in providing funds for research. Membership is only £5 a year, and there are groups throughout the UK."

"I've heard of the PDS."

"I also belong to Yappers; - short for Young, Alert Parkinsonians, Partners & Relatives. It's a branch of the Society for people who are of working age when Parkinson's is first diagnosed. We meet a few times a year. It keeps us in touch. Here, again, I've made new friends and because we share the same condition, talking together helps us to see ourselves in a new light. There is a quarterly magazine here, too, with interesting features. It's very important that people with Parkinson's do not see themselves in isolation. We can help each other.

You'd be amazed at the number of people who, although they don't have Parkinson's themselves, are members involved in committee work. They give their time and effort freely. Without them the society would not run as well. There are groups throughout the country, and I can recommend membership."

"It's good to know that there are such groups about. I'll tell Bron about it. It would do her good to be a member."

69

"Well, we really should be going. We only dropped in for a while, but we've been here for a good time. I have enjoyed our chat."

"Good. I hope you haven't been bored with my tale of woe or found it too difficult understanding me. My speech makes communication difficult. "

"I haven't been bored; far from it. It's good to know how life is for others. There are so many people who have complex conditions of one sort or another. I'll do my best to make my friends aware of this complaint. I'll certainly think before I become irritated when standing at a cash desk behind someone who's holding up the queue, seeming to be struggling. I now know that there may be a jolly good reason. I'll also think twice before assuming a person is drunk because he or she appears to be drunk. We're sometimes too quick to jump to conclusions, aren't we?"

"True. I have often been thought of as drunk, even when I'm stone cold sober. I've had many an accusatory glare."

"Come on, Meg. We really must go. Thanks for the coffee, Val. It was good to see you again. All the best. I've got words of encouragement for my sister now. I'll call in again to see you and maybe Bron will come with me. She'd like to see you, I know."

"That would be nice. I shall look forward to it. I can't tell you how much I've enjoyed your company. It's been therapeutic for me. Goodbye to you both and take care! Keep in touch."

Val Bowden

As I See Myself

To all intents and purposes, I'm no different.
I'm seen as being normal, seen as fine.
My outward self signals that *I'm well*
but my inward self is private; it's all mine.

For years I have been changing from a person once
as fit and well as could have been desired,
but although my image still looks good -
middle-aged grace - now I'm always tired.

The changes are so cruel, so strange,
they are difficult to describe -
I have moments that reduce me to a state
of depression. But I won't subscribe

to this. I will not let it get the best of me.
I will stay in control. I will not sink
into the depths of worrying what I'll be.
Why me? I think.

My body is so strange at times, not moving as it should,
it has a mind to do whatever it chooses.
At times it doesn't do what *I* want;
at others, it performs: *it* chooses.

My legs often seem a ton or more,
moving them so difficult to achieve,
feet rooted to the ground, fixed,
weighted down. It's hard to believe

the tension - as hard as tempered steel,
or a rock which has settled over years.
To rid the body of such restraints
seems impossible, they're fixed, as certain as tears.

Still, my brain is not yet in pain,
though it, too, has changed; it's not alert,
not as quick to work, not as nimble -
now the world can hurt.

My confidence is an empty shell,
lacks heart, it's dead.
My spirit, which not so long ago was strong and full,
is now a shadow; holds the dread

of things unknown, and being in company of others;
the dread of being forced to make decisions.
The dread that people will see a body uncontrolled,
that I'll be a cause for derision.

I've known stages of desperation,
feelings of despair. I could be lost.
They're real, all pervading, cruel,
they possess me like a boat, wave-tossed.

But then I go on, wear a face for the world,
seem no different from the rest; show I'm
quite confident, quite able to get by:
'I'm fine, doing just fine.'

And should I speak my worst fears?
Weigh it up, view the way my life now stands,
the weakness, shaking, twitching, the slowing down.
Shall I give in, depend on others, hold up my hands?

No. I'll count the credits
see beyond the pain.
I have a mind, I have a home, I have a husband,
I have a family; these sustain.

Contributors

Dannie Abse - is one of Wales's leading writers. His novel **Ash on a Young Man's Sleeve** is a classic account of a Jewish boy growing up in war-threatened Cardiff. A former President of the Poetry Society. Dannie Abse's **Collected Poems** is published by Hutchinsons. He edited **Twentieth Century Anglo-Welsh Poetry** for Seren Books who also published his **Intermittent Journals.**

Margaret Atwood - is Canada's most famous writer and one of the best novelists in the language. She began as a poet in the 1960's and Virago's **Eating Fire: Selected Poetry 1965-1995** appeared in 1998. The author of acclaimed novels, including **The Handmaid's Tale** which was filmed. Four of her novels have been short-listed for the Booker Prize, the latest of which, **The Blind Assassin,** won the 2000 Booker Prize.

Barbara Bentley – is a graduate of the Masters in Writing at the University of Glamorgan. Her first collection, **Living Next to Leda,** was published by Seren, from whom her second collection will appear in 2002. She is Head of English and Performing Arts at Wigan & Leigh College.

Carole Bromley –is a teacher from York currently studying for the M Phil in Writing at Glamorgan. Her poems have appeared in a number of journals including *Stand, The Rialto, The North Tabla.* She has also taken first prizes in both the Staple competition and the First Lines Competition 2000.

John Burnside – A prize-winning Scottish poet who lives in Fife and is Writer in Residence at Dundee University. In 1992 **Feast Days** won the Geoffrey Faber Memorial Prize, while his latest collection, **The Asylum Dance,** won the 2000 Whitbread Poetry Prize and was short-listed for the T.S. Eliot prize.

Rosemary Burton – the cover painting **Blue Irises** is one of many paintings produced by Rosemary, a former teacher at Cowbridge

74

School. Her work is now exhibited widely in Wales and is included in the web gallery _www.gallery4wales.com_

Gillian Clarke – is one of the most popular poets in schools and colleges in the UK. She also teaches on the Glamorgan Masters. A former Chair of the Welsh Academy and founding President of the Ty Newydd Writers' Centre, Gillian Clarke, since the 1970's, has been the central woman poet in Wales. Her latest collection was **Five Fields.** In 1997 she received the Cholmondeley Award. www.gillianclarke.co.uk

Lynette Craig – is a student on the Glamorgan Masters. She has published poems in _The Jerusalem Review_ and had work included in **The Dybbuk of Delight.**

Tony Curtis – is Professor of Poetry at the University of Glamorgan where he leads the M.Phil. in Writing. In 1985 he won the National Poetry Prize, in 1993 the Dylan Thomas Award and in 1997 a Cholmondeley Award. He has published two books on contemporary Welsh art, **Welsh Painters Talking** and **Welsh Artists Talking** and founded the web gallery www.gallery4wales.com. His ninth collection of poetry **Heaven's Gate** appeared from Seren in 2001 and selected poems, **Dal Confine,** in Italian, from Moby Dick in 2000. www.glam.ac.uk

Amanda Dalton – is a graduate of the Masters in Writing at Glamorgan and currently Education Director at the Royal Exchange Theatre, Manchester. Her first collection **How to Disappear** was short-listed for the Forward First Collection Prize and her radio play **Room of Leaves** was the BBC Prix Italia entry for 1998.

Michael Donaghy – was born in New York, but has been resident in Britain since 1985. His three collections of poetry are **Shibboleth,** which won the Whitbread Prize for Poetry, **Errata,** which won the Ingram Merill Foundation Award and **Conjure,** short-listed for the 2000 T.S. Eliot Prize.

75

Helen Dunmore – is a novelist and poet. She was the first winner of the Orange Prize in 1995 for her novel, **A Spell in Winter.** Her novels include – **Talking to the Dead, Burning Bright** and **Your Crooked Heart** – and she has published many other books for children, short story collections and poetry, including **Bestiary,** which was a PBS Recommendation in 1997.

Peter Finch – is Chief Executive of the Academi, the writer's organisation in Wales. A former manager of the Oriel bookshop and venue, and founder of *Second Aeon,* he has been an influential figure in literary Wales since the 1970's. Author of many collections and a frequent performance poet. Seren published his **Selected Poems.** www.dial.pipex.com/peter.finch

Catherine Fisher – is a poet and prize winning writer for children. She won the 1989 Cardiff International Poetry Prize, the 1995 Tir na n'Og Prize and was short-listed for the 1990 Smarties Prize. www.geocities.com/catherine

Matthew Francis – teaches Creative Writing at the University of Glamorgan. He read English at Cambridge and later did a Ph.D. on W.S. Graham at Southampton. He has published two collections of poetry from Faber, **Blizzard** and **Dragons.** He won the 2000 TLS Poetry Competition. www.glam.ac.uk

Seamus Heaney – is the outstanding poet and poetry commentator of his generation. Born in Co. Derry in 1939 and educated at Queens. He has been the Professor of Poetry at Oxford, and Boylston Professor at Harvard. He won the Nobel Prize for Literature in 1998. His version of **Beowulf** was published to huge critical acclaim in 2000. His new collection, **Electric Light,** appears from Faber in 2001.

Paul Henry – is a free-lance careers advisor and tutor in Creative Writing at the University of Glamorgan. He won an Eric Gregory Award for his first collection, **Time Pieces.** Two further collections, **Captive Audience** and **The Milk Thief,** have appeared from Seren Books.

76

Jeremy Hooker – is Professor of English at the University of Glamorgan. His **Selected Poems** appeared from Carcanet and there have been two more recent books from Enitharmon Press. His criticism includes work on Alun Lewis and David Jones. www.glam.ac.uk

Pamela Johnson – is a graduate of the Glamorgan Masters. She has published two novels from Sceptre, **Under Construction** and **Deep Blue Silence**. A free-lance art curator who lives in Muswell Hill, she is working on a collection of poems.

Stephen Knight – was born in Swansea and read English at Oxford. He won the 1992 National Poetry Prize. He has published three collections of poetry, including **Dream City Cinema** and his first novel, **Mr Schnitzel** was published by Penguin in 2000. A tutor on the M.Phil. at Glamorgan.

Gwyneth Lewis – born in Cardiff and educated at Cambridge, Columbia and Oxford, where she wrote her doctoral thesis on Iolo Morgannwg. Five collections of poetry, three in Welsh and two in English, the last four were short-listed for the Welsh Book of the Year. **Zero Gravity** was a PBS Recommendation in 1998.

Michael Longley – was educated at Trinity College, Dublin. He recently retired from the Arts Council of Northern Ireland. His collection **Gorse Fires** won the Whitbread Prize for Poetry. Cape published his **Selected Poems** in 1998. **The Weather in Japan** won the 2000 T.S.Eliot Prize.

Roger Mc Gough – is one of the most popular poets in Britain. A member of the pop group Scaffold and one of the triumvirate Liverpool Poets in the sixties, Roger Mc Gough has since published many collections for adults and children and has written plays for stage, tv and radio. Penguin's **Modern Poets No 10 – The Mersey Sound** was the most influential poetry book for the Beatles generation.

Christopher Meredith – teaches Creative Writing at the University of Glamorgan. The author of three novels – **Shifts, Griffri** and **Sidereal Time** and a children's book in Welsh. He has been short-listed for Welsh Book of the Year. His latest collection of poetry is **Snaring Heaven**. www.glam.ac.uk

Robert Minhinnick – is the editor of *Poetry Wales*. Carcanet published his **Selected Poems** and he has written two collections of travel writing, **Watching the Fire Eater** and **Badlands** from Seren. He is an active campaigner for Green Issues.

Andrew Motion – is the Poet Laureate and Professor of Creative Writing at the University of East Anglia. A notable critic and biographer, Andrew Motion is one of the most successful poets of his generation, winning the 1981 Observer Prize. He published **Wainwright the Poisoner** in 2000 and a new collection of poems is forthcoming from Faber.

Paul Muldoon – born in Co. Armagh and worked as a BBC radio producer until he left to live in America. He is currently The Oxford Professor of Poetry and Professor of Poetry at Princeton. Since the appearance of **New Weather** in 1973, Faber have published a dozen books and Paul Muldoon has been recognised as one of the wittiest and intriguing British poets.

Les Murray – is the best known of Australia's poets. He won the T.S. Eliot Prize in 1996 for **Subhuman Redneck Poems** and received the Queen's Gold Medal for Poetry in 1998. In 2001 his new collection is **Learning Human: New & Selected Poems** from Carcanet.

Leslie Norris - was born in Merthyr Tydfil and is recognised as one of the leading poets and short story writers to come from Wales. Seren published his **Collected Poems** and his **Collected Stories**. He is Humanities Professor at Brigham Young University in Utah.

Bernard O'Donaghue – was born in Cullen, Co. Cork in 1945 and still lives there for part of the year. He came to England in 1962 and is now a tutor in Medieval English at Wadham College, Oxford. He writes on medieval and modern poetry and has published four books of poetry, including **Gunpowder (1995)** which won the Whitbread Prize and **Here nor There** (1999).

Lynne Rees – is a graduate of the Glamorgan Masters. She was a prizewinner in the 2000 Cardiff International Poetry Competition. Lynne was born in Port Talbot but now lives in Kent and teaches a Creative Writing class at the University of Kent.

Jo Shapcott – is one of the leading poets and editors of her generation. The only poet to have won the National Poetry Prize twice. O.U.P. published **My Life Asleep** and her latest collection is **Her Book** from Faber. She has recently held a visiting writers chair at the University of Newcastle.

Owen Sheers – won a Gregory Award and published, to critical acclaim, his first collection, **The Blue Book,** from Seren in 2000. He was born in Fiji, but brought up in Wales and educated at Oxford and the Creative Writing program at UEA.

Anne Stevenson – is an American poet, educated at Michigan and Radcliffe, though born in England and later resident there for many years. Her critical biography **Bitter Flame: A Life of Sylvia Plath** was published in 1989 and the latest of her many collections of poetry **Granny Scarecrow** was short-listed for the 2000 T.S. Eliot Prize.

Theodore Weiss – is one of the most distinguished American poets. Emeritus Professor at Princeton, he has published over a dozen collections. His **Selected Poems 1950-1995** appeared from Triquarterly Press in 1995. His wife Renee and he edited **Contemporary Poetry,** Princeton U. Press in 1975. Theodore Weiss has suffered from Parkinson's Disease for the last fifteen years

Acknowledgements

Bloodaxe Books publish Amanda Dalton, Stephen Knight & Anne Stevenson

Jonathan Cape publish Michael Longley & John Burnside

Carcanet Press publish Gillian Clarke, Les Murray
& Robert Minhinnick

Enitharmon publish Jeremy Hooker

Faber & Faber publish Matthew Francis, Seamus Heaney, Andrew Motion ,
Paul Muldoon & Jo Shapcott

Hutchinson publish Dannie Abse

Oxford U.P. publish Bernard O'Donaghue

Penguin publish Roger McGough

Picador publish Michael Donaghy

Seren books publish Barbara Bentley, Tony Curtis, Peter Finch,
Catherine Fisher, Paul Henry, Christopher Meredith,
Leslie Norris & Owen Sheers

Virago publish Margaret Atwood